Train Music is a venturesome alliance of poetry '
the other onward. The poems are filled with vil
pictures with heart and solicitude – together th

author of *To Paint A Life: Charlotte Salomon* in ᴛʜᴇ ᴊᴀᴢᴢ ᴇʀᴀ

What is it to say, "Train's the music"? Is it the motion? The movement across space? What are the components of its rhythm? In this radiant collaboration—C. S. Giscombe's explorations of various possible paths through poetry and identity, Judith Margolis' deft drawings and collages— Train Music traces the travel and friendship of the alternately colored, Negro, cold-water Negro poet Giscombe and the artist Margolis ("raised amidst Yiddish endearments") across the land by rail, tunneling through histories by word and image. "Poetry's fightin' words" that train the reader for navigating in "the unsounded ocean in that gasp that is life." This collection invites us right on board

TONYA M. FOSTER
author of *A Swarm of Bees in High Court* and *Thingification*

Reading *Train Music,* the collaboration between the African-American poet Giscombe and the Jewish-American artist Margolis ("old friends since Ithaca days . . . never lovers"), I find myself swaying in tune with the train on the curving irregular tracks. The book is an account of the friends' four-day journey from New York to San Francisco. While Giscombe evokes cultural and personal history in the passing geography, Margolis wrestles a moody insomnia with layered collages and drawings of the very landscape that Giscombe catalogs.

The divergent responses of the poet and the artist to their shared experience create a tantalizing and graphic mix of poetry, image, and prose but what feeds the creative explorations of both Giscombe and Margolis is their unknowing. Discovery is deferred and the book flows forward.

GILAH YELIN HIRSCH
artist and Professor of Art at California State Univ. Domingues Hills

Hauntingly exquisite and powerfully prescient, Judith Margolis and C.S. Giscombe's, collaborative, *Train Music* is a tour de force of diasporic poetics. Between destinations, and dreams, desire and displacement, it both literally and figuratively dances through an interwoven collage of identity, history and culture, celebrating the exilic performativity of being.

ADEENA KARASICK
author of *Salomé: Woman of Valor*

Having ridden on trains from the east, having cast stories on tidal bores that push from salt water into fresh, having dodged "the seminar's bad eyes," and finding themselves neither here nor there, but somehow still inside the joke of the idea of race, Giscombe and Margolis compose their travelogue in the present-absence of tender doubt. "Power's always locatable on the other side of the mountain, distant," but Giscombe activates the line and the sequence to articulate poems that range far while simultaneously enfolding near. Margolis answers with sketches that are always more than their figures, because the seen bring their own annotations to their rendering. See that, the artist says. Hear that, the poet says. But they know the trains come and go like italics on the *says*.

FARID MATUK
author of *The Real Horse*

It's the long train ride from New York City to San Francisco—two friends with notebooks, sketch pads, questions, speculations, conversations about poetry wars, race, family and place—four days and nights with eyes and ears open to create a sound track—a kind of railroad music as accompaniment to the vast American landscape that crawls or flashes by.

C. S. Giscombe, the poet, note-taker, maker-of-journeys is also tangled in the conflict of compiling notes for a talk in San Francisco on "white supremacy." Judith Margolis, in juxtaposition, is sketching a series of visuals and notes, drawings and collages that also establish literal locations: her body flying, reclining, or tucked in the sleeper car, "trying to sleep like a normal person," the Chagall-like figures on a rooftop stretching for the moon, the palm trees of California....

But this is just a hint of the complexity and overall context of this wonderful book. Robert Creeley wrote, "nothing is without place/in mind, in physical apprehension." These two artists got that here. *Big.*

BARRY MCKINNON
author of *The Centre*

Train Music is a guide, not only a poem. It is a song, a journal, a biography, and a graphic score. Like a map, its words and drawings trace the journey of two friends crossing the US: C.S.Giscombe's words are verbal images, while Judith Margolis's collages and drawings playfully morph into text, prose and verse alike. Each of the two parts accompany the other, while contrasting the dynamic conversation between a black American and a Jewish American voice.

Giscombe's writing embodies train movement: rhythmical, carefully composed, and, in the spirit of Free Jazz, in almost constant motion, ever changing. It carries the reader through American history, not as taught in textbooks, but through the lens of a black poet who has actually lived it.

Margolis's female-centered drawings stand on their own and express the woman's voice on this journey. They are at times intentionally contrasting, at other times embracing the male written narrative. Margolis's images tell their own stories, literal and abstract (if and when they want to), guiding the reader through the passing landscapes and cities.

Take this ride. It's worth it.

LUISA MUHR

interdisciplinary performer,

Founding Director of Women Between the Arts

A Jewish woman and a Black man, long time friends (but not lovers). Children of the 60's. Self-sustaining adults in the real world. Collaborators.

What can they make together that they can't do alone? Dreams and nightmares. Asking questions and shaking things up.

Two travelers on a journey of friendship looking for creative sparks. Art and life, life and art. Crossing America, awake and asleep.

Waking dreams and sleeping dreams. Keen mental observation combined with intuition.

Giscombe's poetry is like a map, with references worth investigating. Follow the cues. Maps of the heart, maps of the mind, marking time.

Margolis' artwork is a perfect counter point to the writing. Dream-like and rich in color and emotion, giving you clues and a tone, but leaving much to fill in from your own imagination and experiences. This book is all about Train Music. The devil may care or not, but not all sharks are alike.

VICTOR RAPHAEL

inter-disciplinary artist

Train Music is an inspiring synthesis of words and visual images. Friends, African American poet C. S. Giscombe and Jewish American artist Judith Margolis, have seized upon their fascination with train travel in order to create a narrative that is both deeply felt and almost metaphysical in scope. The trains elicit a deep love of what they call "train music," the rhythmic noise and embodied dislocation experienced by riders as they are thrust across space. For the poet, trains are redolent with history—they call up the physical construction of the railroads, the Great Migration, and Jim Crow and its aftermath. Meanwhile, Margolis's drawings, paintings, and collages evoke a different story, paralleling the poem, but not in illustration of it. Her diaristic, and richly colorful artworks depict a mysterious female dreamer as an alternate point of reference for her audience. Taken together, Train Music anchors readers to the specificities of everyday life, but then frees them to fly amidst the percussive meditative sound of the rails.

JOEL SILVERSTEIN

Artist, Co-founder of Jewish Art Salon

In *Train Music*, Giscombe's narrative disjunctions and Margolis' figurative abstractions crisscross at a roundhouse ("I'm not a white girl, you said," "How do I get away with it, you wanted to know") as they cut yard, heading West. For Giscombe, on his way to either "shake things up" or "furnish comfortable words" for a white audience about to hear his lecture on white supremacy, the ironies are hardly unique. Margolis' moody, dark drawings evade easy definition by swaying back and forth, from depictions of a woman asleep in a bed and a woman ring a house as her head to women standing on the roof of a house (upright coffin, empty coffer). Her vertical spirituality (the moon is one of her motifs) serves as counterweight to Giscombe's horizontal zig-zag agnosticism, laying low like the Greenland shark that "runs those *seminars*/ way down under that ice,/ unconsumable/ maybe/ alive a thousand years/ down there." *Train Music* celebrates the survival of two artists selected by two histories for extermination. Together though, Giscombe and Margolis dance to the singing wheels of their cross-country trains, "A foot in one car, / a foot in another, passing from one to the next one."

TYRONE WILLIAMS

author of *As iZ*

TRAIN MUSIC

TRAIN MUSIC

WRITING / PICTURES

C. S. GISCOMBE
JUDITH MARGOLIS

OMNIDAWN PUBLISHING
OAKLAND, CALIFORNIA
2021

Cover photo credit: *Crossing Signal,* Judith Margolis

Cover typefaces: Program
Interior typefaces: Program, Baskerville

Cover and interior design by adam b. bohannon

Library of Congress Cataloging-in-Publication Data

Names: Giscombe, C. S., 1950- author. | Margolis, Judith, author.
Title: Train music : writing, pictures / C.S. Giscombe, Judith Margolis.
Description: Oakland, California : Omnidawn Publishing, 2021. | Summary:
"Train Music chronicles the 2017 four-day railroad trip (New York to
California) of poet C. S. Giscombe and book artist Judith Margolis, old
friends. Giscombe was returning home to address an all-white audience on
white supremacy; expatriate Margolis, usually solitary and itinerant,
was visiting the country of her birth, drawing scenery and collaging
insomniac night visions. Journeying, conversing, arguing, sharing
memories, they document a complex and volatile American landscape, one
at once geographical and historical, one holding specific implications
for the lives of both. Margolis and Giscombe chart their own passage
through all that, through a dangerous and puzzling world that-too
often-"passes as normal." Train Music is the insistent and unlikely
shape that the two sensibilities achieve"-- Provided by publisher.
Identifiers: LCCN 2021002387 | ISBN 9781632430885 (paperback)
Subjects: LCGFT: Poetry.
Classification: LCC PS3557.I78 T73 2021 | DDC 811/.54--dc23
LC record available at https://lccn.loc.gov/2021002387

Published by Omnidawn Publishing, Oakland, California
www.omnidawn.com   (510) 237-5472
10 9 8 7 6 5 4 3 2 1
ISBN: 978-1-63243-088-5

CONTENTS

TRAIN MUSIC

NEW YORK TO EMERYVILLE-SAN FRANCISCO ON THREE TRAINS.

The *Pennsylvanian* runs between New York City and Pittsburgh, stops in Newark, Trenton, Lancaster, Harrisburg, Altoona, Johnstown, and Greensburg. "Train crews on the *Pennsylvanian* come in from Harrisburg and lay over in Pittsburgh. The train service attendant works all the way from New York."

Connection to the *Capitol Limited* at that train's crew change point in Pittsburgh, the *Capitol Limited* having originated in Washington. Train crosses Ohio in the dark—dawn at Toledo—and calls at the Indiana stations (Waterloo, Elkhart, South Bend) before arriving in Chicago at 8:45, Central Standard Time.

The *California Zephyr* leaves Chicago every afternoon for the coast.

Among the passengers: Judith Margolis and C. S. Giscombe, old friends since the Ithaca days; contrary, humans. Never lovers. "Raised amidst Yiddish endearments," she said; and sometimes calls herself St. Soleil. New Jersey girl. Awake, asleep. A poet (both West Indian and Mississippi Negro), he would address migration itself, the family having settled in southern Ohio. "We have been pragmatic," said he.

Travel Dates: 24-27 November 2017
Tickets (x 2): Reserved Coach from NYP to Pittsburgh; Sleeper from Pittsburgh to Chicago; Sleeper from Chicago to Emeryville-San Francisco.

Friday, 24 November 2017

1.

Last bits of dream of the night before in which I'd been invited to "come see the river" and then, later, was swimming in a tidal pool or in the sea, and the light was such as it is. Sour stomach, pool of words to speak being a cold-water Negro into being.

                Sour
stomach upon rising, up early
               because of the music—harsh
    and the voices in it only circular, or
                      nearly repeating, or the same
          peaks achieved and achieved
again—in the airshaft.

Sour stomach and early but having come down the street then (St. Nicholas Avenue), in fact, singing. On the way that morning to the subway—that train—singing down St. Nicholas, how "I used to love to watch her dance that old Grizzly Bear," sang, "she's gone to Frisco, gonna dance it there."

("Back east"—sister's, in Harlem, Thanksgiving—and now *en route* back home, to California.) Sour stomach upon rising, old song, Christmas just around the corner.

2.

Your question, asked on the Pennsylvanian, *had to do with first memory, with the initial place— not location—of self, the place* beside the world, *you'd said. No* place *but the powerful boy, myself, cut out—all of a sudden—from this or that, separate from all else.*

The *head* of a Negro. Study that.

Maybe it was *besides the world.*

Late morning. New York Penn, Newark, Trenton, then into the
    30th Street station—

Philadelphia—by 12:15.

Electric locomotive from NYP to Philly, having

crossed New Jersey behind that boy,

"under catenary."

Stories—cautionary tales—had swept through childhood.

Keep your head above water.

Surprise sometimes—a history of shark presence, even

in "fresh waters," the figure on which such tales were based.

Train leapt the *filthy Passaic*—"mindless," "nesting place," "haunt,"

"contagious"—or seemed to.

Train crossed the Delaware, the Raritan, etc.

Shark had come right up Matawan Creek—out of Raritan
    Bay—and ate four.

Pearly white on the History Channel.

Change the power at 30th St., one diesel to haul us—from there—
    on out to Pittsburgh.

sultry blue fading beyond desk to night
the silhouette of the mountain
range a (female) form suggesting female
breasts & belly
& thighs-
voluptuous and
sound

a man bent over a pickety cart loaded
dust cleaning supplies & pink -
stray clothes -

3.

Traveling. The schoolboys might say, *some traveling subject.*

Having agreed to address "white supremacy" upon my return to
    California.

At a "Roundtable."

Symptom of what?

(Typical power.) My agreeable nature, fidgeting over the tracks.

On the street, in stations. Unspoken of. Standing water in ditches

(by the tracks).

Feign my shock?

Expect me, something said.

Feign my shark.

Water just standing there saying nothing.

Remember me, said something else.

Inure me, boys, to hardship and to the "peculiar apparition."

Bless public affairs and public issues.

I work around the place.

Gender me, boys, and have me "dawdle" over the tracks.

Daniel Webster threw an inkwell at the devil's shadow on the
    wall, because it was *talking.*

Mistake my silence.

4.

Leave Lancaster, then stop at Harrisburg to change the crew.

Narrows on the jolting Juniata, through that place (along that
    river).

One black conductor qualified west of Banshee, that territory.

(Through that place, alongside the river.)

Came to Lewistown Junction, PA and took on passengers there.

Say that, diesels say that. That. Say,

stride's different than turpentine camp.

Came up to Lewistown Junction, took on some passengers there

What's *that*?

Pennsylvania shout, boys! Pennsylvania shout!

5.

"How do you get away with it?" you said.

(Judith said.)

Put some sand down, they said, so we can get underway; and
   then again
   —more sand—

up at the summit.

In the report to the public I was said to muse on this or that.

You'd mistaken a lover for his music, you said. Somewhere.

Look again, look again.

(Waste time, idle, loaf around, boys, as you all are wont to do.)

They discover supremacy over and over again.

Wheels slip, wet steel.

Always the shock to see it in the water, fresh like a newborn baby.

Bad eyes, but hold the snout up.

Ice in the ditch.

5.5

Which kind of shark do you-all want to be?

Handsome face in the mirror.

(Second question.)

Train's the music.

Train sings.

Train just forgets about your eyes.

Train sings.

6.

Train towns. Locomotive shops. Famous, in the literature,
    is Lower Trainswitch.

A hundred miles—old song for how far you can hear.

Old Altoona: iron bridge over the railroad to climb and then
    walk across

(on the way to high school).

Mountlake Terrace Jazz Ensemble played "Harlem Airshaft," up

on YouTube, all-white high school band.

Parallel tracks twisted through town.

(After which we crossed the Alleghenies in the dark, no snow or
    lights to mark it.)

"The train is teeming with people's thoughts," you said.

On hills—or wet leaves in autumn—the flanged wheels will just spin.

Sand's a metaphor, too.

Helper six-axle locomotives at Cresson just to push the train over
    the Horseshoe Curve.

(There's work—

in the train stations and in the sleeping cars, and there's kitchen

work and waiting tables and that, and online, where

it's *jobtitle=Attendant*, respondent said, "they turn you into a
    train slave"

—we're to do.)

Summit Tunnel, the twin bores at Gallitzin.

Negro Mountain's summit is the highest point
    in the Commonwealth.

"Autumn Leaves," a standard.

Rich Mountlake's out by Seattle.

Put sand in your pipe and smoke it.

Pleasure though—
at the lip of the dining car—
in being so greeted,

that.

Music opens *that* up.

Having crossed the odiferous Fens once—concrete bridges, sluice-gates—
singing Billy Stewart songs, songs (old songs even back then) by Martha
Reeves and the Vandellas.

West of Banshee—where the green grass grows—a white man
stepped on a black man's toes.

Music, it's grim like that, sometimes.

(Having followed the tracks north out of Ely, losing them
somewhere—I was cycling

—because of the road diverging, as it does.)

Not the music I'd *heard.*

7.

Poetry wars? you asked, in the waiting room.

Two anthologies, I said

(that evening, Pittsburgh).

White poets squared off, white guys in print, on paper:

Grove Press, them—I said—and some other imprint.

Empty Pittsburgh waiting room.

The wild white chaps fought the white crafty lads—

long ambiguous looks cast from both campsites—tooth and claw.

Such as it was, *the war*

was always there—everybody

pretty-boy for the camera— *but we didn't go to it.*

Pittsburgh, Amtrak.

Poetry's fightin' words.

Question's more interesting—almost always—than the answer.

Trying to not watch but—*check it out*—the Negro criminals on
    big TV screens

everywhere.

Well-lit, the waiting room. Watch while you wait.

No matter to the analogy.

Cap Limited due close to midnight.

8.

Prepared my remarks *en route* but, later, at the Roundtable, those
   got no traction.

I wanted the Fisk Jubilee Singers to do "Two Trains Runnin'."

Pink faces in the Golden State.

Facts of white supremacy—*said I*—*are simple and local and it's no
new thing: to wit, please* see *how big the* social *really is and how*—*for that
one colored kid in (say) the college auditorium*— *overwhelming the social
is* because *of the unspoken* ordinariness *of the* well-met. *That is, the
colored kid doesn't try to come "back" after the seminar*—*benign as well it
may have appeared to be for you-all*—*is over.*

No response.

"The runaway train came down the track/ the sand was on an'
   the lever back."

(Others spoke of the various presidents—their duplicities—and
   the distant wars.)

Look for me in the funny papers.

(Real title's "Still a Fool.")

Protect the train, boys.

Power's always locatable on the other side of the mountain,
   "distant,"

some mean-faced old kangaroo over there.

Just the one cold-water fellow (myself) "on the Roundtable" at the
   fancy event—filigreed

lounge, down among the well-heeled, district of theaters and
   such, "university life," shouting

distance from the Barbary Coast (so called, "ironically").

The colored professor's role—according to university *legend—is to "shake things up." Or (in keeping with wider,* social *custom) furnish comfortable words.*

Them? Those two?

"Caucasian melodies," said Uncle Mike. Fail that and this too.

Ostentatiously bad year—post-election—here in Babylon had
    preceded that afternoon,

but the seminar's been *flying,* fact over fact, for a while.

Train music?

Or how she sang—*If it ain't sea, it's land/ If you ain't praised, you're panned/ If it ain't fresh, it's canned/ Gotta be this or that.*

I'm just notches on a curve—stations and control points—or *still*
    just out of step, fish

out of the cold, cold water.

9.

Ohio, late. Train music—you wanting me to hear "Hallelujah"
   in Yiddish, it

being the *sound* of the language, you said, spoken by parents, etc.

The rectangle of the oncoming door sways and down below
   and visible

—when you're on a train walking, say, to the dining car—

is *in fact* the moving ground. A foot in one car,

a foot in another, passing from one to the next one.

10.

"Nice" whites call me from Canada still—bad years for
   everyone—to talk.

They catch up with me, they say.

"We caught up with him in Prince Rupert," they said
   on CBC Daybreak.

(I know where the Negroes entered Canada.)

Klan doesn't like Jews, you said, cause they're white on the
   outside but black on the inside.

They'll catch up with you on the road. Colored man in a fur coat.

You called some train music up on YouTube, even late in Ohio, in the night season.

Hallelujah.

How did I get away?

Sharks following the train.

How did I get to be this way? What did I do?

St. Leonard came out of Westmount.

Greenland sharks come down the St. Lawrence sometimes,
   past Tadoussac,

into the Saguenay Fjord, where people sometimes catch them
   "whilst ice-fishing."

They go for centuries, outliving the angler (usually) easily.

"The species is doubtless abundant throughout the polar seas."

Westmount's 15 minutes by car from *le pont Samuel-De Champlain.*

I wanted the Fisk Jubilee Singers to do "O Canada."

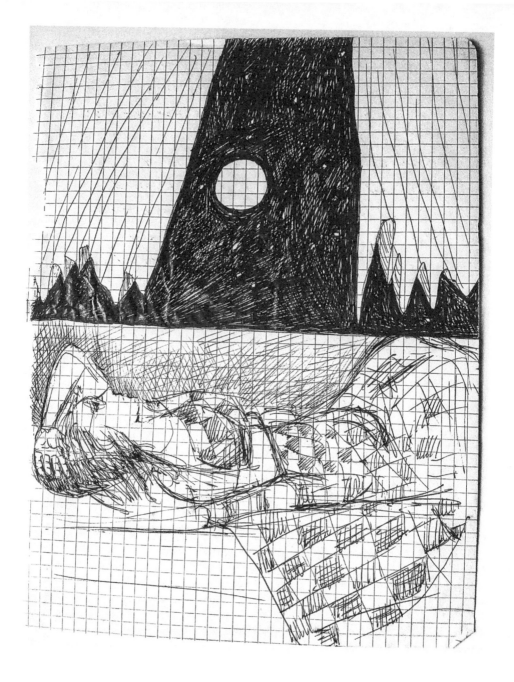

11.

Beatrix—my old friend—had a "Boston wife."

Just that.

Childcraft book, *Animal Friends and Adventures*, had one boy

ride the China Clipper and had another, "a modern boy,"

take the train to New York.

Train's mystery, song says. More than that.

Pretty boys on the masthead. Perching birds, plain-beaked.

Chalky figure-head. No one says a thing.

Shark's out ahead, train follows the shark.

12.

Time? No, powerful boy, distance—talk to yourself (I said),
    answer Judith.

Speak to her question, powerful boy.

Maybe the first dream, in which God was an Army tank,

patrolling the trenches, which were infinity, "world

without end," patrolled by God.

God's on patrol, doesn't forget.

We'd got to Ohio before I thought of it (the answer).

Forget that noise.

(*One* of the answers.) Fear the *infinite*.

Age?

Three, or four.

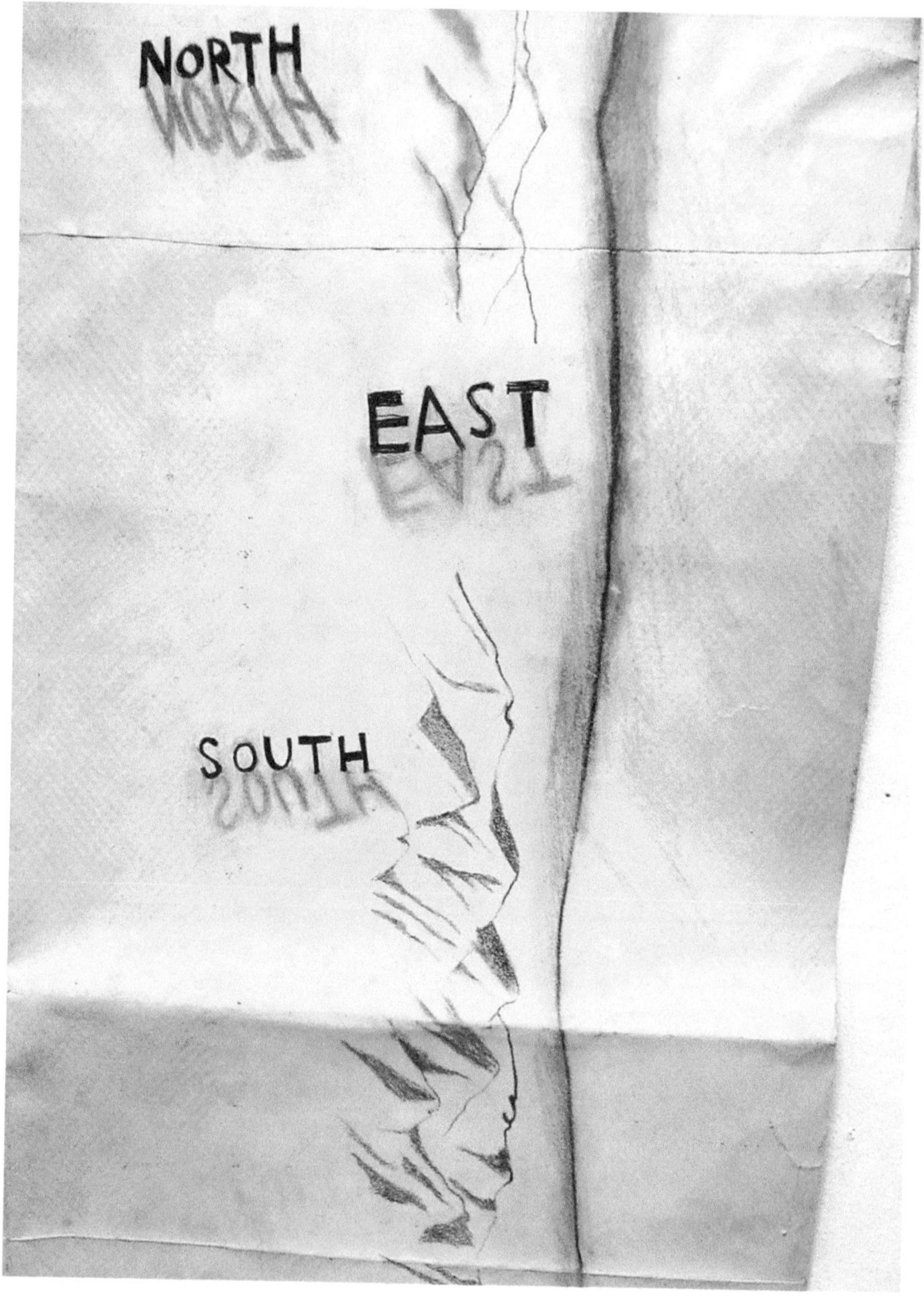
NORTH
EAST
SOUTH

13.

"The porter is the colored servant on the train."

That unsounded ocean you gasp in is life; those sharks, your foes; those spades, your friends; and what between sharks and spades you are in a sad pickle and peril, poor lad.

Beat that boy, Mister Ralph said.

14.

Later—in another story—the Big Brown Bear had got in trouble with bees due to his taste for honey and those bees chased him *and he hid in the water with just his nose sticking out which they found and stung repeatedly.*

Our one old uncle changed his name, said that he'd been
    a "waif of the empire."

Relative to travel.

Consider that, sound that that makes.

Who do you think's looking at you?

Subject me to that, boys. Dance in iron shoes.

Consider *betterment.* Consider the Indiana Plan. Consider Hoosierdom. Bear down.

Consider the Lead Service Attendant.

Waterloo, Elkhart, South Bend.

Who's minding the hive if the skunk's at the picnic?

It was the railroads invented standard time.

I'm not a white girl, you said.

15.

Long layover in Chicago, walking to the Art Institute—pallid collection of
African pieces downstairs and the dull Stickley examples on the Mezzanine,
these all in comparison to the young Satyr with the theater mask, oversized
headpiece, customized face of an old man—and then walking back,
in time.

16.

Consider the answer.

I was beside myself.

Brother Karl said that that thing, taught to all the chubby-cheek
locomotives in the school,

to hurt the Negro and avoid the Jew, that

that was the lesson, that that, sir, was that.

How you gonna win, when you ain't right within? Ms. Hill had asked.

17.

Zephyr crossing the Mississippi on the new draw-bridge
  at Burlington!

Dance the bare dance.

*Dining car divides the sleepers from the coaches. Judith and I will approach it
from the rear, I noted. Coach passengers line up at the other end.*

> *Behind someone*
*complaining that she was feeling "claustrophobic" and that the "car
attendant" was "not sympathetic," this on the* Zephyr.

Come see that river.

Big decision— should I draw
my breakfast before I eat it?
gratitude—
Seeing the stars + moon from
my bed, very turbulent ride—
I like the nighttime with
my private rocking bed—

I'm being a bit of a freak wanting
expecting to be friendly + "get
to know" the other people who I
sit with in the dining car—
So Chuck came by for breakfast—
he totally seems like a friend
already"

OttumwA, IOWA

Misreported—that it was a great white that came upstream and ate those people back in Matawan. Rather, it was a bull shark, *diadromous*, a requiem shark, as easily at home—when need be—in rivers as in the open water. The boys pulled one out of the Father of Waters at Alton, three-hour drive south of Burlington, shark having swum right past St. Louis and East St. Louis too!

"Race you to the river!" said the fine black horse to the locomotive.

The west wind, esp. as personified.

Wasn't snowing, wasn't going to snow either but *cold* all up
    and down the prairie and

it'd be cold, cold as Cottage Grove Avenue, across

which would come—now and again—the Prairie shout. That is,
    here and there,

'cross Iowa where the *tall* grass grows, the diesel horn. Sound
    come cold

as Christmas. *I'm* sour as can be at the smoke stops.

Dream on, I'd say.

*Granddad had driven from St. Louis to see us in Cincinnati and Dayton
and had skirted a field full of "those triple-K boys" who were convening just
outside Miamisburg, Ohio (town named for the river), 1960 or so, Granddad
laughing twenty years later at the memory. Dixie Highway, old U.S. 25.*

Train wears a big old mask.

Train's in disguise.

(Train's disguise.)

Train on the runway like a boa constrictor.

Colored servant rule applies. "No safe seats," I'd say

in the California ballroom but, unlike

old times elsewhere, it was soon forgotten.

Watch italics, boys.

Train striding up on California like a bad sport.

Some of us, though, had learned how to do and / or how

to keep it in on the side,

white speech, say, on the streets south of the Art Institute, *how*

to make a look an omen

(Miss Brooks had said).

Besides, the world.

"Head of a Negro" having been the study for "Watson
and the Shark,"

that Negro upright and *ambiguous* in the boat.

Copley's Negro, "subject to interpretation."

Look at that shark, look at him with his great nostrils all flared!

Do you know to speak?

*Mme. Martichou asked, "Is the boy"—young Watson—"going to be
saved?" And answered, in her own next sentence: "The black figure seems
in doubt."*

Do you know how to run?

Roundhouse is where they keep the locomotives.

In the Middle Ages—wrote Mister Philpot—*the Devil was portrayed as
a dimwitted mean buffoon, easy to outsmart.*

Train muscle. Swing it around.

Ride the heated dance, Mister Bear.

I don't do diversity work, the colored poet had said to me on the
telephone at SFO.

18.

I want to be honest, everyone said.

Direction's elusive.

(Some little lank-headed fool would stick up his hand and that's
 what he'd say.)

Nope, train just going west across the wide Missouri, then
 on across Nebraska.

Auditorium here, auditorium there.

Order me a black-and-tan.

"*Suitability and propriety,*" brothers, rule the roost.

(Consider the ambiguity *of being "right within.")*

Never, brothers, never say *"supreme."*

Ordinary,

California nights.

And single malts and fine colleges,

and good food on good china.

I'll take a dram.

Platte's "a mile wide and a foot deep."

OK, I said.

19.

Reverse move into Denver.

It just paces the train, effortless grace on its white horse.

We already knew that, barked the stray locomotive.

From outside the roundhouse door.

(Train backing slow. Reverse move through the Denver yards,
    bang over the switches.)

How do I get away with it, you wanted to know.

No story either way—backwards or forward—but
    a well-made poem, stepping lively.

Black horse says, Race me to the river.

Black hoss grins, *Disable me.*

Make me make you feel comfortable with all that, all my levers.

Miscellaneous me.

Dismount me.

Make me.

(All my loves.)

Locomotive said, *You ain't had enough train music for all those lifetimes?*

Red foxes live in the Denver yards, visible from the *Zephyr.*

You ain't had enough train music *yet?*

Flash of beauty—*seen*—inbetween the tracks.

"I thought I would fall of weariness," said Invisible Man.

Keep up. Vary it. Capture it.

Mistah Fox, showing up again, Mistah Fox showing up
    out in the yard.

Dissuade me.

"Them's years," said the Grandfather.

and tries to

exorcise demons

20

*Current catchers / pantographs on the arriving RTD airport train, Denver
Union Station, next track. Passengers in Denver, on the platform, marching.
Young people taking the train in tight jeans.*

*Our check-pants uncle in the
dining car—cigarette face man, narcissist—said, we like to feel 'em marching
right and left of us; share me, he said because life's that way, feeling's another
way.*

To be a rider—a remora fish as it were—and not know
   you're on the *Zephyr*. That is,

to be carried forward by an unseen agency—call it Mariah, call it

what your pocket can bear. The feathers in your nest
   come from heaven.

Well-met, brothers, well-met.

Railroad's a shiny thing to a crow. See it a mile off,
   big flange wheels.

Crow-bar Denver.

Railroad Bill, Railroad Bill / Never worked and never will.

Shout in the white noise, train. Blow the space into decoration.

*Maybe, as one would reply to an inquisitive mind, to an inquiry, concoction is
what you rub against the skinny chest that's against your own. Money, honey.
Good clothes. Is this OK? Wave it around.*

Or like the big black bird that ate the French fry off the white
paper plate on the patio, having swooped in like a Negro eagle.

If the devil's in the details who's that in the woodpile?

Who'd want to be a bad sport?

Resist me, train. Concoct me.

GRAND JUNCTION

GRAND JUNCTION wasn't so grand anymore.

European style Train station -
but disintegrating from neglect and the forlorn disappearance
of a way of life.

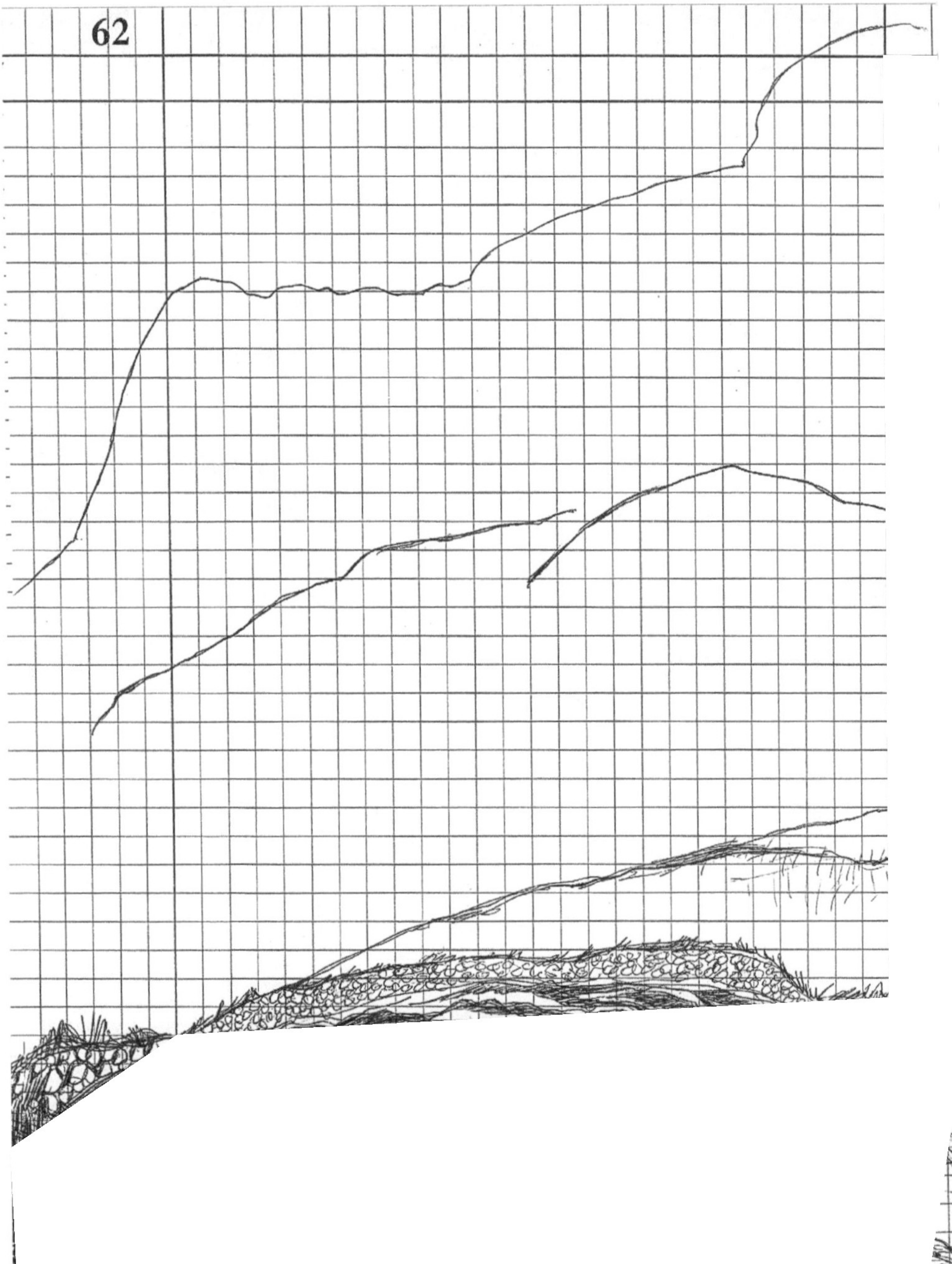

in Colorado on
AMTRAK NOV 26 2017

63

21.

Grafitti'd hoppers in a field, the three tracks next to this one
    on which sit boxcars and tank cars.

Other flash of red—like a blackbird's shoulder patch—

as we go over a grade crossing. Colorado,

past Grand Junction, past Glenwood Springs,

train towns.

How then, will we get away?

Having slept through Moffat Tunnel after meditating,

after having left Denver, having tacked up the hill from that.

You-all call the Colorado River "Moon River" for the rafters' practice

(when the *Zephyr* steams by).

Two older red Cadillacs parked helm to stern. One 60s, one 50s, the latter
with bulbous taillights and humped curve of the trunk—the boot, they say in
the Fens—and the former being, simple enough, finned.

Four bald-headed

eagles across

the Colorado River.

In trees.

The colored
girl in the poetry class had had to explain (for the class and its teacher) the
joke, referenced in the poem, in which the perceived Cadillac was actually a
Pontiac. Poem had made reference to its speaker's father's car, "which he knew
was a Pontiac," unlike the Negro in the joke.

Not the home place. What'd you come here for? people ask.

Between *here* and the deep blue sea!

Here we are, dear.

Step lively, train music.

Und der Haifisch, der hat Zähne/ Und die trägt er im Gesicht…

Keep out of sight of the seminars' bad eyes.

22.

Poetry wars. Train music, as for me? Just inevitable. This is, itself,
   some music. Double score.

A binary proves its distance; a binary proves distance is out there;
   one-two, buckle my shoe.

Double tracked is one way in each direction.

Shut the door some more, Charlie Brown.

Trump me.

The getaway is sweet—compartments in the fat years, otherwise

it's the fellowship of the coaches.

The sea is teeming with shark fins, isn't it?

A train covers distance. (A train covers the distance.)

There's a bear in *my* bonnet.

"Even the tambourinists"—Miss Sherley Anne said—"and those
who shake the bones coax/ beauty from nothingness and / desire."

Dance the floor bare.

Low fin on the Greenland shark rarely breaks the surface, if

ever, in the schemes of things. They eat bears, dogs, and reindeer
   and are

"seldom seen."

23.

Open trace.

Open, trace.

Tell me who was that Grizzly
(Grizzly Bear)
Oh Jack o' Diamond was that Grizzly
(Grizzly Bear)
Oh Jack o' Diamond was that Grizzly
(Grizzly Bear)

"The song appears to be a tangent statement about events that are not clearly spelled out," someone said.

"Did you ever hear of a white man named Christmas?"

day

grave   cancelled

urday

yed at   what

r by   (30) eer/Hotel

self   3   st

                                    Jeff's party

t line of

en — the

up stuf to keep disks

up for Crash Plan

24

River talk, at dinner, in the dining car. (At table, Gale and Jim—she having previously "been married to a black man"—mentioned the Walker River, which rises in the Sierra Nevada, the California side. Valley stream, she said, cattle graze it. He was ill, silent over the plated chicken and the salad, but roused for that. *Most herds*—he whispered—*are 36 cows*.)

Crossed out of Colorado, early evening, after dark (it being near winter).

Helper, Utah—just over the line—"decked out" in colored lights up and down the storefronts, for Christmas. Tiny downtown, single street. Brick box train station. Named so because—like Cresson, PA—it's where they kept the extra locomotives, the ones to help you up the steep road, get you to the top of the hill, sweet Jesus.

"Utah Railway coal train battles the grade towards Soldier Summit" (5,364 views).

"Amtrak 192 Leads Amtrak #5 Over Soldier Summit, 6/7/09" (8,215 views).

Zephyr moanin' across the state.

In Utah, they'd noted, in explanation, how we "were *said* to have been less than fully valiant in the premortal battle against Lucifer and, as a consequence, were restricted from priesthood and temple blessings."

My italics, boys.

Number 5's the westbound, number 6 the eastbound.

Train towns.

Long layover—service stop—in Salt Lake City.

Those Utah Railway coal runs—night trains—

through the station at some speed, moaning also. Midnight

before we started up again.

Later, still awake in the sleeping car, saw

the Peppermill Casino—still open, lights still on at 2 am—

from the train, across a field, as we crossed into Nevada, rolled

on out of the Beehive State.

Train music's the devil.

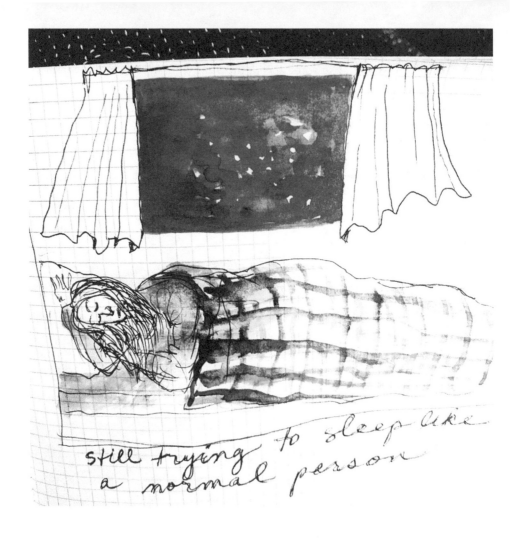

still trying to sleep like
a normal person

25.

Very young woman of indeterminate color, said she was
    "from Jackson,"

five-week-old baby sucking Ranch dressing off her finger.

Empty Nevada. Little extra, everywhere.

Lunch in the dining car! Young woman but big-boned!
    Mince my oaths!

Zephyr gliding past the World-Famous Mustang Ranch then

—Jiminy Christmas!—come to Reno!

Having started out down old St. Nicholas itself on the way to
    catch the *Pennsylvanian*.

(Just in from Harlem, I'd bought myself a croissant
    at Penn Station and another one for you…)

A black woman once saw the mother of Christ and drew her in charcoal on
the court- house wall. . .

Train music.

The Harlem Goat—in the song—coughed up three red shirts
he'd eaten off a clothesline and, that way, "flagged the train,"
which was *fast approaching*.

Other versions had it being "Bill Grogan's goat"; or "Riley's goat."

Wake me up, up there.

Send a boy up with a red rag to stop the dreaming.

Send the Irish back uptown, then send the Dutch.

What kind of work do you do? someone asked.

Fast Truckee River alongside the track. California nigh.

Ashbery's dead—third guy in the wild man book's alphabetical list—but Bernadette Mayer continues to write. My new friend Q and old friend Erica Hunt.

God will send a boat, a helicopter, even an extra train flying a white flag, to pull you from your fate.

"White is an extra train not found in the timetable."

Kick off your shoes, train mule.

Roll up your sleeves, powerful boy, climb down off the tank
    and save 'em.

Sneaking up on the Golden State.

You send me / Honest you do.

Or on some other dexterity.

Roll up your trousers and get to work.

"Further Respondent sayeth not."

deeper blue/tourquoise   white

paler blue/yellow

pale pink

blue green / orange
shadow   sun reflected

BROWN ORANGE

green (area house soft)

green

green

lavender grey

green

26.

Dear Judith,

I'd have you hear my father, when he and I were talking once, and I had asked if he'd been able—in the 1950s—to book a sleeping car berth on the overnight train to his childhood home in Birmingham and he said, laughing, "They didn't like *selling you one, but they* would.*"*

C.

27.

Had gone back to England and lived there for a while.

Went to Canada, lived there again and again.

Smoke stop in Sacramento, half empty by that afternoon, then
   alongside Suisun Marsh, way past

the *wreck* made of the song—*you never heard a girl sing it*, she said,

meaning *before*—because of how she'd sung it and swung it beyond

the marsh, she and *her fellas*, spending

"like sailors," and then

the old drawbridge

at Martinez:

came to that, crossed it.

Shark's just the example.

Salt-water and the fresh water meet, hail fellows,

shake hands under the Roundtable.

But how the *Zephyr* rocked along Carquinez Strait—the tracks
   parallel the water, *curve* where it does!

      Over in Africa they call it the Zambezi shark, shark
up in that river.

        Over here—meaning,
   this time, way

      out in "harbourless" Canada—it's
        the Greenland shark, that's who
         runs those *seminars*

   way down under that ice,
unconsumable,

  maybe alive a thousand years
        down there.

Someone told me how somebody else—on

the internet—had posted how
he'd seen a great white once
(from this train)
from the old bridge
at Martinez, down among the container ships.
I said that I doubted it.

Learning to live alone with only the moon for company

END

ILLUSTRATIONS

All art and photographs are by Judith Margolis
Unless otherwise stated, all images are courtesy of the artist.

NOTES/ CITED

HEADNOTE

BurghMan. "Re: Crew Change Points In Pittsburgh, Pa???" Accessed 1 May
2020. http://forums.railfan.net/forums.cgi?board=NS;action=display;num
=1192082379;start=0.

SECTION 1

Jackson, Jim. 1928. "'This Morning She Was Gone' Jim Jackson (1928) Blues
Guitar Legend." Accessed 1 May 2020. https://www.youtube.com/
watch?v=ossjwknLIsg .

SECTION 2

Roethke, Theodore. 1998. *The Far Field*. New York: Bantam Dell Publishing
Group.

Williams, William Carlos. 1917. *A Book of Poems: Al Que Quiere!*. Boston: The Four
Seas Company.

—. 1923. *Spring and All*. Paris: Contact Publishing Company.

"Site of the New Jersey Shark Attacks of 1916/ Matawan, New Jersey."
Accessed 1 May 2020. https://www.atlasobscura.com/places/matawan-
new-jersey-shark-attack-of-1916.

The authors wrote:

> With previous deadly attacks in Beach Haven and Spring Lake, New
> Jersey, the shark made its way north and down a freshwater creek
> in Matawan, New Jersey on July 12, where it would attack and kill
> 12-year-old Lester Stillwell and 24-year-old Stanley Fisher within an
> hour of each other. Matawan hadn't prepared itself for attacks like
> other shoreline towns in New Jersey, as they were so far inland along a
> freshwater creek.

Korzeniowski, Józef Teodor Konrad. 2005. *Serce Ciemności*. New York: W.W.
Norton, Norton Critical Editions.

SECTION 3

Benet, Stephen Vincent. 1993. *The Devil and Daniel Webster and Other Writings*.
New York: Penguin Classics.

Blake, William. 1789 (?). "The Proverbs of Hell." Accessed 1 May 2020. https://
poets.org/poem/proverbs-hell .

Blake wrote:

> The fox provides for himself, but God provides for the lion. Think in the
> morning. Act in the noon. Eat in the evening. Sleep in the night. He who
> has suffer'd you to impose onhim knows you. As the plow follows words,
> so God rewards prayers. The tygers of wrath are wiser than the horses of
> instruction. Expect poison from the standing water. You never know what
> is enough unless you know what is more than enough....

Melville, Herman. 2013. *Moby-Dick*. New York: Signet; Reprint edition.
  Melville wrote:
  > Nor even in our superstitions do we fail to throw the same snowy mantle
  > round our phantoms; all ghosts rising in a milk-white fog- Yea, while
  > these terrors seize us, let us add, that even the king of terrors, when
  > personified by the evangelist, rides on his pallid horse.
  >
  > Therefore, in his other moods, symbolize whatever grand or gracious
  > thing he will by whiteness, no man can deny that in its profoundest
  > idealized significance it calls up a peculiar apparition to the soul.
Stevens, Wallace. 1922. "The Emperor of Ice Cream." Accessed 1 May 2020.
  https://www.poetryfoundation.org/poems/45234/the-emperor-of-ice-cream.
  Stevens wrote:
  > Let the wenches dawdle in such dress As they are used to wear...
The Poetry Foundation's linked-in "Poem Guide" ("The chilly heart of a
  whimsical poem," accessed 2 May 2020; https://www.poetryfoundation.
  org/articles/70138/wallace- stevens-the-emperor-of-ice-cream) wrote only,
  of "wenches"—in terms of *meaning*—,"which can mean female servants, as it
  does here, or prostitutes in other contexts."
O.E.D. says, qualifying the usage as "U.S.": "In America, a black or colored
  female servant; a negress"; and "A colored woman of any age; a negress or
  mulattress, especially one in service. (Colloq.)"; and (from the Boston Gaz.
  of 1756), " 'Tis said the Fire was occasioned by a Negro Wench carrying a
  Quantity of Ashes." (Oxford English Dictionary, s.v. "wench." Accessed 2
  May 2020. https://www-oed- com.libproxy.berkeley.edu/view/Entry/22778
  9?rskey=Sfaxg4&result=1#eid.) Dawdle.

SECTION 4

See James P. Johnson, "Carolina Shout." https://youtu.be/
  ENhEVM1aQNk?t=20.

SECTION 6

"Amtrak Employee Reviews for Attendant." Accessed 1 May 2020. https://
  www.indeed.com/cmp/Amtrak/reviews?fjobtitle=Attendant .
Crampton, Gertrude and Tibor Gergely. 2001. *Tootle*. New York: Golden Books;
  Reissue edition.
"Essentially Ellington 2018—Mountlake Terrace Jazz Ensemble I—
  Harlem Airshaft." Accessed 1 May 2020. https://www.youtube.com/
  watch?v=Ktur6_vzLQw .
West, Hedy. "500 Miles." Accessed, 1 May 2020. https://www.youtube.com/
  watch?v=rwnNdqpCF8Q .

SECTION 7

Allen, Donald. M. 1960. *The New American Poetry*. New York: Grove Press.
Hemingway, Ernest. 2017. *The Short Stories of Ernest Hemingway: The Hemingway
  Library Collector's Edition*. New York: Scribners.

SECTION 8

academic_rasta. 2011. "Babylon." Urbandictionary.com. Accessed, 1 May 2020.
[A]cademic_rasta wrote:

> "Rastafarian word referring to The State and The System: it refers equally
> to the British Empire which engineered the slave trade and to the modern
> oppressive governments of the USA and her allies, as they are considered to
> be one and the same imperialist evil. It's believed that the Babylon actively
> seeks to exploit and oppress the people of the world, especially people of
> African descent. It's believed that the Babylon forbids the smoking of ganja
> because this sacred herb opens men's minds to the truth…."

Fitzgerald, Ella. "Gotta Be This or That." Accessed 1 May 2020. https://www.
youtube.com/watch?v=nDLtKg_PSvM. "Gotta Be This or That" is the theme
song for the live quiz show "Minds Over Matter," Sundays 7-8 (Pacific Time),
KALW-Radio, 91.7, San Francisco.

Randolph, Vance. 1992. *Unprintable Ozark Folksongs and Folklore: Roll me in your arms,
Volume 1.* Fayetteville: University of Arkansas Press.

Stoller, Mike. 1991. "Jerry Leiber: Remembering One Of Rock's
Great Songwriters." Accessed 1 May 2020. https://www.npr.org/
transcripts/139967351.

Waters, Muddy. 1951. "Still a Fool." Accessed 1 May 2020. https://www.youtube.
com/watch?v=Ss3mmkngYZI .

SECTION 9

Kahn, Daniel. 2017. "Leonard Cohen's 'Hallelujah' in Yiddish." Accessed 1 May
2020. https://www.youtube.com/watch?v=XH1fERC_504 .

SECTION 10

Castro, Jose I. 2011. *The Sharks of North America.* New York: Oxford University
Press.

SECTION 11

"Animal Friends and Adventures." 1949. *Childcraft: Animal Friends and Adventures –*
Vol. 4. 14 vols. Chicago, IL: Field Enterprises.

Melville, Herman. *Bartleby the Scrivener; Benito Cereno; Billy Budd, Foretopman.* 1997.
New York: Book-of-the-Month Club.

SECTION 13

Childcraft: Animal Friends and Adventures. 1949.

Ellison, Ralph Waldo. "'Beating That Boy.'" *New Republic,* 22 October 1945.

Melville, Herman. *Moby Dick.* 2013.

SECTION 14

Duplaix, Georges and Gustaf Tenggren. 1947. *The Big Brown Bear.* New York:
Little Golden Books.

Korzeniowski, Józef Teodor Konrad. 2005. *Serce Ciemności.* New York: W.W.
Norton.

SECTION 16

Hill, Lauryn. "Lauryn Hill—Doo-Wop (That Thing) [Official
   Video]." Accessed 1 May 2020. https://www.youtube.com/
   watch?v=T6QKqFPRZSA .

Shapiro, Karl. "University." Accessed 1 May 2020. https://www.
   poetryfoundation.org/poetrymagazine/poems/22722/university .

SECTION 17

Brooks, Gwendolyn. 1991. *Blacks*. Chicago: Third World Press.

Copley, John Singleton. "Watson and the Shark. (1778)". Accessed 1 May 2020.
   https://www.nga.gov/collection/art-object-page.46471.html .

Crampton, Gertrude and Tibor Gergely. 2001. *Tootle*.

Martichou, Élisabeth. "Bridging the Gap between Self and Other? Pictorial
   Representation of Blacks in England in the Middle of the Eighteenth
   Century/ Les Noirs dans la peinture anglaise au milieu du dix-huitième
   siècle: une tentative pour rapprocher le moi et l'autre?" *Revue Lisa*. Accessed
   1 May 2020. https://journals.openedition.org/lisa/8735?lang=en.

McCormick, Harold W. and Tom Allen with Captain William E. Young.
   Shadows in the Sea (Illustrated). Chilton Book Company: Philadelphia—New

York—London, 1963.

The authors wrote:

> …Sharks appear in several British coats-of-arms. Sir Brook Watson, Alderman of London, lost a leg from the bite of a shark in the harbor of Havana. The incident was magnificently portrayed by the painter John Singleton Copley in his famed "Watson and the Shark." But that wasn't enough for Watson. Created baronet in 1803, he assumed for a crest a demi-triton, grasping a trident and repelling a shark in the act of seizing its prey. The crest of the family of Aiolton has a shark's head regardant, swallowing a Negro…

Philpot, Thomas Barton III. *God with Us: Christ in the Synoptic Gospels: from the Coming of John the Baptist and the Genealogy of Jesus Through His Healing of Legion, the Demoniac.* 2010. No Location: Xlibris Corporation, Publisher.

"Sharks in Illinois." *In-Fisherman* [online]. Accessed 1 May 2020. https://www.in-fisherman.com/editorial/sharks-in-illinois/154988 .

SECTION 18

English Language & Usage Stack Exchange. "What was 'well met!' supposed to mean?" Accessed 1 May 2020.

https://english.stackexchange.com/questions/35144/what-was-well-met-supposed-to-mean .

> [U]ser57716 wrote:
>
> This is an old expression dating back to the 16th century. The descriptive phrase "well- met," had (and still has) connotations of suitability and propriety. It's based on a different meaning of "meet," an adjectival/adverbial usage indicating something is literally or figuratively the right size for a given situation.

Lomax, John A. and Alan Lomax. *American Ballads and Folk Songs.* 2013. North Chelmsford, Massachusetts: Courier Corporation.

SECTION 19

Ellison, Ralph. *Invisible Man.* New York: Random House, Inc; Fourth Edition (1980)

SECTION 20

Cohen, Norm. 2000. *Long Steel Rail: The Railroad in American Folksong.* University of Illinois Press.

Korzeniowski, Józef Teodor Konrad. 1993. *Lord Jim. New York: Penguin-Random House, Everyman's Library.*

SECTION 21

"Die Moritat von Mackier Messer (Kurt Weill, Bertholdt Brecht, 1928)." Zugriff am 1. Mai 2020. http://www.nthuleen.com/teach/lyrics/mackiemesser.html.

Rahimtoola, Samia. In conversation, c. 2015.

SECTION 22

Williams, Sherley Anne. 1980. "Letters from a New England Negro." *The Iowa Review.* Volume 11, Issue 4.

SECTION 23

Courlander, Harold. 2019. *Negro Folk Music U.S.A.* Mineola: Courier Dover Publications.

Faulkner, William. 2011. *Light in August.* New York: Vintage; 1st Vintage International edition.

SECTION 24

"Amtrak 192 Leads Amtrak #5 Over Soldier Summit, 6/7/09" (8,215 views). Accessed 1 May 2020.https://www.youtube.com/watch?v=2bnMkKnnASE .

Church of Jesus Christ of Latter Day Saints. "Race and the Priesthood." Accessed 1 May 2020.https://www.churchofjesuschrist.org/manual/gospel-topics-essays/race-and-the- priesthood?lang=eng.

"Utah Railway coal train battles the grade towards Soldier Summit" (5,364 views). Accessed 1 May 2020. https://www.youtube.com/watch?v=MKG0Mx60W_k .

SECTION 25

Cohen, Norm. 2000. *Long Steel Rail: The Railroad in American Folksong.* University of Illinois Press.

Franklin, Aretha. "Aretha Franklin—You Send Me" Accessed 1 May 2020. https://www.youtube.com/watch?v=HQNJTmyPdnw.

Hayden, Robert. "Middle Passage." https://www.poetryfoundation.org/poems/43076/middle- passage . Accessed 1 May 2020.

Hayden wrote:

Jesús, Estrella, Esperanza, Mercy:

> Sails flashing to the wind like weapons,
> sharks following the moans the fever and the dying;
> horror the corposant and compass rose.

> Middle Passage:
> voyage through death
> to life upon these shores.

SD70M-2Dude. "Locomotive Flags." Accessed 1 May 2020. http://cs.trains.com/trn/f/111/t/253366.aspx

SD70M-2Dude wrote:

As Tree68 said, White is an extra train not found in the timetable, Green is for a train which has been split into sections (usually because there is too much traffic for one train) and all sections except the last must display green flags/lights, and Red is the marker for the trailing end of a movement.

Toomer, Jean. 1923. *Cane.* New York: Boni & Liveright.

SECTION 26

Giscombe, C. S., Jr., M.D. In conversation, c. 1992.

SECTION 27

Brathwaite, Kamau. 1973. *The Arrivants: A New World Trilogy*. New York: Oxford
   University Press.
   Brathwaite wrote:

> Never seen
> a man
> travel more
> seen more lands
> than this
> poor
> path-
> less harbourless
> spade...

Fitzgerald, Ella. "Ella Fitzgerald Mack the Knife Live in Berlin Audio Flac."
   Accessed 2 May 2020. https://www.youtube.com/watch?v=qs3oCqdkNuc

ABOUT THE AUTHORS

C. S. Giscombe's poetry books are *Prairie Style, Giscome Road, Here,* etc.; his book of linked essays (concerning Canada, race, and family) is *Into and Out of Dislocation.* His recognitions include the 2010 Stephen Henderson Award, an American Book Award (for *Prairie Style*) and the Carl Sandburg Prize (for *Giscome Road*). *Ohio Railroads* (a poem in essay form) was published in 2014 and *Border Towns* (essays on poetry, color, nature, television, etc.) appeared in 2016. He teaches at the University of California, Berkeley, where he is the Robert Hass Chair in English. He is a long-distance cyclist.

Essayist / artist Judith Margolis draws on the spiritual when confronting the political. Her work aims to celebrate, question, berate and poke a finger at how utterly unpredictable and unintelligible life is. Devoted to a life-long feminist consciousness, radical educational philosophy of de-schooling society, and commitment to counter-culture social activism, she maintains an extreme engagement with and ambivalence about religious tradition, especially, but not exclusively Judaism. She is sometimes healed by how things look.

Most recently her illustrated memoir *Life Support: Invitation to Prayer*, was published by Penn State Press for their Graphic Medicine Series. Her company, Bright Idea Books, publishes fine, limited edition artist's books.

Train Music
by C. S. Giscombe & Judith Margolis

Cover photo credit: *Crossing Signal*, Judith Margolis

Cover typefaces: Program. Interior typefaces: Program, Baskerville.

Cover and interior design by adam b. bohannon

Printed in the United States
by Books International, Dulles, Virginia
On 55# Glatfelter B19 Antique
Acid Free Archival Quality Recycled Paper

Publication of this book was made possible in part by gifts from
Katherine & John Gravendyk in honor of Hillary Gravendyk,
Francesca Bell, Mary Mackey, and The New Place Fund

Omnidawn Publishing
Oakland, California
Staff and Volunteers, Fall 2021

Rusty Morrison & Ken Keegan, senior editors & co-publishers
Kayla Ellenbecker, production editor & poetry editor
Rob Hendricks, editor for *Omniverse*, marketing, fiction & post-pub publicity
Sharon Zetter, poetry editor & book designer
Liza Flum, poetry editor
Matthew Bowie, poetry editor
Anthony Cody, poetry editor
Jason Bayani, poetry editor
Gail Aronson, fiction editor
Laura Joakimson, marketing assistant for Instagram & Facebook, fiction editor
Ariana Nevarez, marketing assistant & *Omniveres* writer, fiction editor
Jennifer Metsker, marketing assistant